Grades 1–3   Cello

Improve your sight-reading!

Paul Harris

Contents

FABER *ff* MUSIC

Introduction

Being a good sight-reader is so important and it's not difficult at all!
If you work through this book carefully – always making sure that you
really understand each exercise before you play it – you'll never have
problems learning new pieces or doing well at sight-reading in exams!

Using the workbook

1 Rhythmic exercises

Make sure you have grasped these fully before you go on to the melodic
exercises: it is vital that you really know how the rhythms work. There
are a number of ways to do the exercises, several of which are outlined
in Stage 1. Try them all out. Can you think of more ways to do them?

2 Melodic exercises

These exercises use just the notes (and rhythms) for the Stage, and are
organised into Sets which progress gradually. If you want to sight-read
fluently and accurately, get into the habit of working through each
exercise in the following ways before you begin to play it:

- Make sure you understand the rhythm and counting. Clap the
  exercise through.
- Know what notes you are going to play and the fingering you are
  going to use.
- Try to hear the piece through in your head. Always play the first note
  to help.

3 Prepared pieces

Work your way through the questions first, as these will help you to
think about or 'prepare' the piece. Don't begin playing until you are
pretty sure you know exactly how the piece goes.

4 Going solo!

It is now up to you to discover the clues in this series of practice
pieces. Give yourself about a minute and do your best to understand
the piece before you play. Check the rhythms and your hand position,
and try to hear the piece in your head.

Always remember to feel the pulse and to keep going steadily once
you've begun. Good luck and happy sight-reading!

Terminology:
Bar = measure

The golden rules

A sight-reading checklist

Before you begin to play a piece at sight, always consider the following:

1 Look at the time signature and decide how you will count the piece.

2 Look at the key signature and think about how to finger the notes.

3 Notice patterns – especially those based on scales and arpeggios.

4 Notice any markings that will help you convey the character.

5 Count at least one bar in.

When performing a sight-reading piece

1 Keep feeling the pulse.

2 Keep going at a steady tempo.

3 Remember the finger pattern of the key you are in.

4 Ignore mistakes.

5 Look ahead – at least to the next note.

6 Play musically, always trying to convey the character of the music.

Look at each piece for about 30 seconds and try to feel that you are *understanding* what you see (just like reading these words).

Don't begin until you think you are going to play the piece accurately.

With many thanks to Charles Ellis for his invaluable help.

© 2012 by Faber Music Ltd
Bloomsbury House 74–77 Great Russell Street London WC1B 3DA
Music processed by MacMusic
Cover and page design by Susan Clarke
Cover illustration by Drew Hillier
Printed in England by Caligraving Ltd
All rights reserved
ISBN10: 0-571-53697-2
EAN13: 978-0-571-53697-9

Grade 1 **Stage 1**

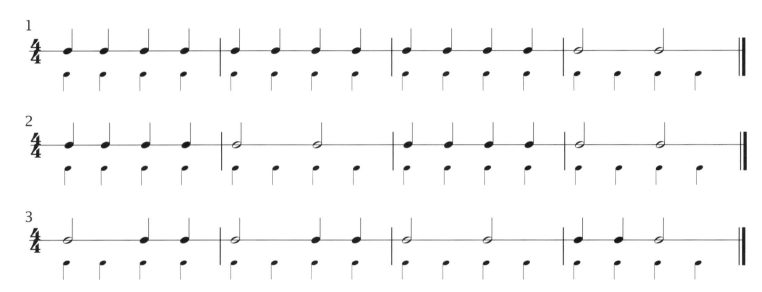

G major $\frac{4}{4}$

Rhythmic exercises

The rhythmic exercises are really important. Always practise them carefully before going on. There are different ways of doing these exercises:
- Your teacher (or a metronome) taps the lower line while you clap or tap the upper line.
- You tap the lower line with your foot and clap or tap the upper line with your hands.
- You tap one line with one hand and the other line with the other hand on a table top.
- You tap the lower line and sing the upper line.

Before you begin each exercise count two bars in – one out loud and one silently.

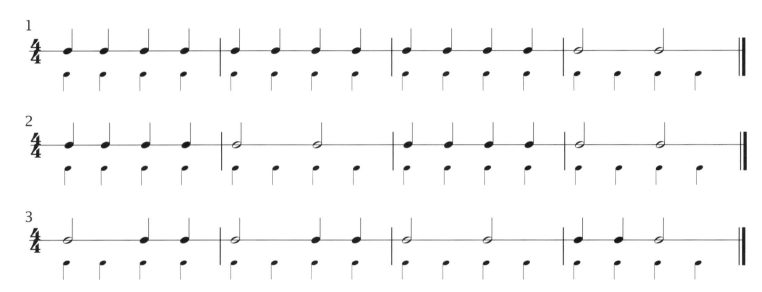

Melodic exercises

Set 1: Exploring the open G string

Hear each exercise in your head before you play it.

Set 2: Exploring the notes on the G string

Set 3: Exploring the G string notes plus open D string

Set 4: Exploring the G major scale

Prepared pieces

1 How many beats are there in each bar? What will you count?

2 What is the key? Play the scale.

3 What do bars 1 and 4, and 2 and 6 have in common?

4 Play a G (the first note) then hear the piece in your head.

5 How will you put some character into your performance?

Marching

1 How will you count this piece?

2 Tap the rhythm then (tapping the pulse) hear the rhythm in your head.

3 Are there any repeated rhythm patterns?

4 Compare bar 1 with bar 4.

5 How will you put some character into your performance?

Sleepily

Improvising

Make up your own piece (it can be as long or short as you like), beginning with this pattern. Make sure you keep the pulse steady.

Now make up your own piece in G major, using any patterns you like.

Going solo!

Remember to prepare each piece carefully before you play it.

Grade 1 Stage 2

Rhythmic exercises

Always remember to count two bars in.

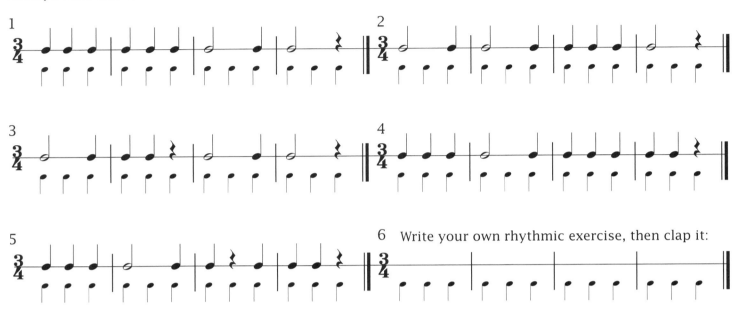

Melodic exercises

Set 1: Exploring D major with ⅘

Set 2: Exploring small leaps

Set 3: More ⸱

Set 4: Longer examples

Prepared pieces

> **1** What is the key? Play the scale. Say the names of the notes in the piece.
>
> **2** What will you count? Tap the rhythm of the piece.
>
> **3** Find the two leaps in the piece. What do they have in common?
>
> **4** Think about how you will finger the piece.
>
> **5** How will you put some character into your performance?

Flowing

> **1** How will you count this piece?
>
> **2** Tap the rhythm then (tapping the pulse) hear the rhythm in your head.
>
> **3** Are there any repeated rhythm patterns?
>
> **4** How many leaps can you find? How will you finger each?
>
> **5** How will you put some character into your performance?

Waltz-time

Improvising

> Make up your own piece (it can be as long or short as you like), beginning with this pattern. Make sure you keep the pulse steady.
>
> Now make up your own piece in ¾ and D major.

Going solo!

Remember to prepare each piece carefully before you play it.

Grade 1 Stage 3

Dynamic markings

♪♪ 2/4

Rhythmic exercises

Always remember to count two bars in.

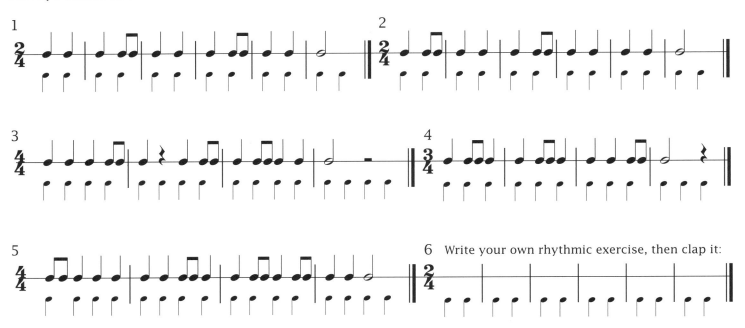

Melodic exercises

Set 1: Exploring 2/4 and ♫ on the same note

Set 2: Introducing ♩♩ on different notes

Prepared pieces

> **1** How many beats are there in each bar?
>
> **2** Do any bars contain the same rhythmic patterns?
>
> **3** Tap the rhythm then (tapping the pulse) hear the rhythm in your head.
>
> **4** How will you put some character into your performance?
>
> **5** Play a G (the first note) then (tapping the pulse) hear the piece in your head.

Heavily

1

> **1** What is the key? Play the scale. Say the names of all the notes.
>
> **2** What will you count? Tap the rhythm of the piece.
>
> **3** Do any bars contain the same rhythmic patterns?
>
> **4** What do the two dynamic markings tell you?
>
> **5** Play a D, then hear the piece in your head, with the dynamic markings.

Dancing

2

Improvising

> Make up your own piece (it can be as long or short as you like), beginning with this pattern.
> Make sure you keep the pulse steady.
>
>
>
> Now make up your own piece in $\frac{2}{4}$.

Going solo!

Remember to prepare each piece carefully before you play it.

Grade 2 Stage 1

Rhythmic exercises

Always remember to count two bars in.

Melodic exercises

Set 1: Introducing 2-note slurs

Set 2: Introducing 2-note slurs in ♫

Set 3: Slurring ♩ and ♫

Set 4: More slurred ♩ and ♫

Prepared pieces

1 What will you count? Tap the pulse and hear the rhythm in your head.

2 What is the key? Play the scale and arpeggio in a dancing style.

3 Can you spot any repeated patterns – rhythmic or melodic?

4 What is the interval between the first two notes called? To which pattern do they belong?

5 How will you put character into your performance?

1 How will you count this piece? Hear the pulse in your head and tap the rhythm.

2 In which key is the piece? Play the scale and arpeggio in a singing style.

3 The first two notes belong to the arpeggio – how many other patterns are there from the arpeggio?

4 How many bars share the same rhythm as bar 1? How is bar 3 similar to bar 1?

5 How will you put character into your performance?

Improvising

Make up your own piece (it can be as long or short as you like), beginning with this pattern. Decide on a mood or character before you begin.

Now make up your own piece in G major – use any patterns you like.

Going solo!

Remember to prepare each piece carefully before you play it.

Grade 2 Stage 2

C major

Rhythmic exercises

Always remember to count two bars in.

Melodic exercises

Set 1: Introducing C major upper octave and ♩.

Set 2: Exploring C major lower octave and ▬

Set 3: ♩. and ▬ in other keys

Prepared pieces

> **1** What is the key of this piece? Play the scale and arpeggio in a flowing style.
>
> **2** Can you spot any repeated patterns – rhythmic or melodic? Are there any scale or arpeggio patterns?
>
> **3** Study the last two bars for a few moments then play them from memory.
>
> **4** What will you count? Tap the pulse and think the rhythm, then tap the rhythm and think the pulse.
>
> **5** How will you put character into your performance?

> **1** Think the bowing through in your head.
>
> **2** Can you find a sequence of four notes that belong to the D major arpeggio?
>
> **3** Count in your head and tap the rhythm.
>
> **4** Play the first note and try to hear the piece in your head.
>
> **5** What gives you clues to the character of this piece?

Improvising

> Make up your own piece (it can be as long or short as you like), beginning with this pattern. Decide on a mood or character before you begin.
>
>
>
> Now make up your own piece – include some longer notes and rests.

Going solo!

Remember to prepare each piece carefully before you play it.

Grade 2 Stage 3

Rhythmic exercises

Always remember to count two bars in.

Melodic exercises

Set 1: Introducing A natural minor

5 Write your own rhythmic exercise, then clap it:

Set 2: Exploring 3rds

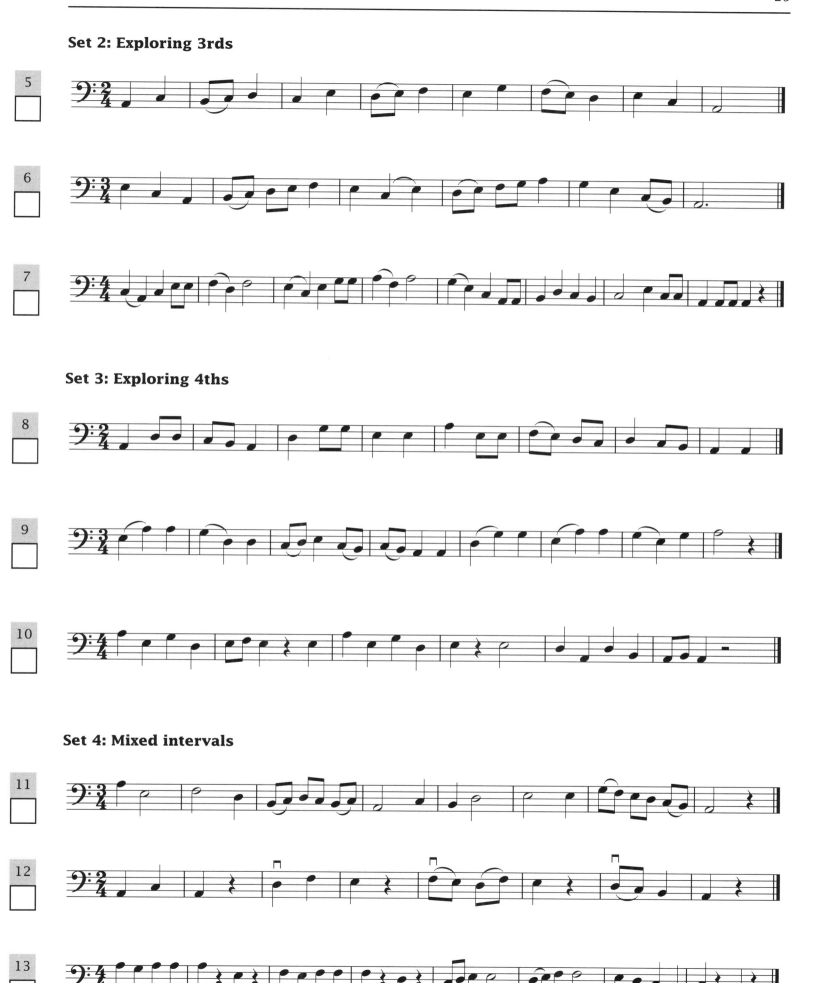

Prepared pieces

> **1** What is the key of this piece? Play the scale and arpeggio.
>
> **2** Can you spot any repeated patterns – rhythmic or melodic? Are there any scale patterns?
>
> **3** Think about the dynamic levels.
>
> **4** What will you count? Tap the pulse and think the rhythm, then tap the rhythm and think the pulse.
>
> **5** Play the first note and try to hear the piece in your head.

1

> **1** What is the interval formed by the first two notes? Is there another example of this interval?
>
> **2** What is similar about bars 1 and 2? Are there any more similar bars?
>
> **3** Tap the pulse with your foot and the rhythm with your hands.
>
> **4** Play the first note and hear the piece through in your head.
>
> **5** How will you put character into your performance?

2

Improvising

> Make up your own piece (it can be as long or short as you like), beginning with this pattern. Decide on a mood or character before you begin.
>
>
>
> Now make up your own piece in A minor – use any patterns you like.

Going solo!

Remember to prepare each piece carefully before you play it.

Grade 3 **Stage 1**

A major

Ties

Rhythmic exercises

Each set of exercises read **downwards**. In set 2, feel the tied notes strongly, but don't play them.
In the dotted rhythm in set 3 you should still feel the 'tied' note, even though it has become a dot!

Melodic exercises

Set 1: Introducing A major and simple ties

Set 2: Exploring ♩.♪ in 4/4
Try no.5 as three separate exercises, then play it all the way through.

Set 3: Exploring ♩.♪ in 3/4
Try no.8 as three separate exercises, then play it all the way through.

Set 4: Mixing ties and ♩.♪

Prepared pieces

> 1 What is the key of this piece? Play the scale and arpeggio.
>
> 2 Can you spot any scale or arpeggio patterns? Name the patterns.
>
> 3 Compare bars 1–2 with bars 3–4 and 7–8.
>
> 4 Tap the pulse and think the rhythm, then tap the rhythm and think the pulse.
>
> 5 Play the first note and hear the piece in your head, including musical expression.

> 1 In which key is this piece? Play the scale and arpeggio.
>
> 2 How many repeated ideas can you find?
>
> 3 Tap the pulse with your foot and the rhythm with your hands.
>
> 4 Think through the fingering.
>
> 5 How will you put character into your performance?

Improvising

> Make up your own piece (it can be as long or short as you like), beginning with this pattern.
> Decide on a mood or character before you begin.
>
>
>
> Now make up your own piece in G, D or A major – use any patterns you like.

Going solo!

Remember to prepare each piece carefully before you play it.

32

Grade 3 Stage 2

F major and Bb major

Rhythmic exercises

Always remember to count two bars in.

Melodic exercises

Set 1: Introducing simple ♩♪♪♪

Set 2: Introducing F major and ♪♪♪

5

6

7

Set 3: Introducing B♭ major and ♪♪♪

8

9

10

Set 4: Different patterns and keys

11

12

Prepared pieces

1 Look through this piece. Do you feel you understand it?

2 Look carefully at the patterns: rhythmic and melodic. How much is based on scale and arpeggio patterns?

3 Play the scale *f* and arpeggio *mp*.

4 Now think carefully about the bowing.

5 Play the first note and hear the piece in your head, including musical expression.

1

1 In which key is this piece? Play the scale and arpeggio *mf* then *p*.

2 How many patterns can you find?

3 Tap the pulse with your hands and the rhythm with your foot. Now swap!

4 Think about the fingering in bars 1 and 6. What is interesting about these bars?

5 How will you put character into your performance?

2

Improvising

Make up your own piece (it can be as long or short as you like), beginning with this pattern.
Decide on a mood or character before you begin.

Now make up your own piece in F or B♭ major – use any patterns you like.

Going solo!

Remember to prepare each piece carefully before you play it.

Grade 3 **Stage 3**

**D and G minor
Staccato and
pizzicato**

Rhythmic exercises

Always remember to count two bars in.

Melodic exercises

Set 1: Introducing

Set 2: Revising A natural minor

Set 3: Introducing D minor and staccato

Set 4: Introducing G minor and pizzicato

Prepared pieces

> 1 In which key is this piece? Play the scale and arpeggio.
>
> 2 Think carefully about the rhythm. Are you certain you know how it goes?
>
> 3 Play the piece in the rhythm, but just using the notes of the arpeggio.
>
> 4 Now think about the bowing.
>
> 5 Play the first note and hear the piece in your head, including musical expression.

> 1 In which key is this piece? Play the scale and arpeggio.
>
> 2 How much of this piece is based on scale patterns?
>
> 3 Think through the fingering – especially in bars 3 and 5.
>
> 4 Tap the pulse with one hand and the rhythm with the other. Repeat, swapping hands.
>
> 5 How will you put character into your performance?

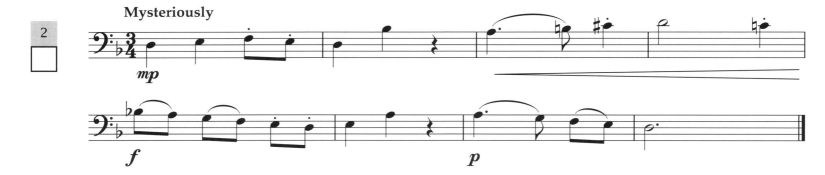

Improvising

> Make up your own piece (it can be as long or short as you like), beginning with this pattern.
> Decide on a mood or character before you begin.
>
>
>
> Now make up your own piece in G or D minor – use any patterns you like.

Going solo!

Remember to prepare each piece carefully before you play it.